BUILD A BUTTERFLY
AND OTHER GREAT LEGO® IDEAS

Contents

Fantasy land 4

A fantasy house 6

Cube Village 8

Fences and pathways 10

A waterfall 12

Fantasy river 14

Fantasy creatures 16

Tree slide 18

Tree-house 20

A castle wall 22

More castle walls 24

Castle walls (continued) 26

Castle features 28

Acknowledgements 32

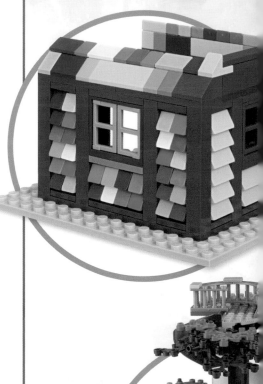

Book breakdown

This book shows lots of inspiring model breakdowns to help you discover ideas and techniques for your own models, but the entire book is broken down, too. There are many different types of pages designed to help you build up your own amazing LEGO® world, section by section, model by model, brick by brick.

Coloured bars, like the one below, run along the top of pages to let you know what kind of page you're reading.

Page number   Page type

Section name

Here are all the different types of pages you'll find in this book:

How to build

Watch one model develop from start to finish on these pages, with helpful building advice at every stage.

What else can you build?

Once you've seen how to build one model, discover different ways of using similar techniques and ideas in your own models.

Expanding your world

Don't stop now! Once you've built a few models, why not add more to your world? These pages give ideas for building extra models and scenery.

Showstoppers

These pages show off the biggest or most interesting ideas in this book. Look at them in detail and use the ideas to build your own showstopper models.

Fantasy Land

Meet Alice. No, not that Alice! This Alice is just an ordinary girl who likes to escape her everyday world by dreaming up a colourful and imaginative place. The moment she walks across this old stone bridge, Alice is in a strange new land filled with all her favourite story-book characters. Help Alice to create the objects, places and animals of her extraordinary fantasy land – and add your own creative spin to them, too!

A fantasy house

None of the colours in this curious little cube-shaped house quite seem to match up! Fantasy buildings are fun to build, even when you don't have lots of pieces with the same colours. You can use whatever colours you like when you're imagining it yourself.

START HERE

If you don't have a big plate, make one out of several smaller ones

The first row of pla is indented one stu from the edge

The rows end two studs from the open edge

1 ⟩ Base plate

Start with a big, square base plate. Place a row of two-stud-wide plates near the edges of three sides, and then a one-stud-wide row of plates on top of that.

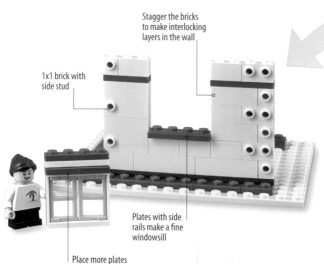

Stagger the bricks to make interlocking layers in the wall

1x1 brick with side stud

Plates with side rails make a fine windowsill

Place more plates with side rails on top of the window

2 ⟩ Think sideways

Use one-stud-wide bricks to start building a wall on top of the tallest plate layer. Position bricks with sideways-facing studs on the ends as shown in the picture. Leave a gap for a window, too.

If you can, make each window's colours different from the other two

1x1 and 1x2 tiles attach sideways to the studs

3 ⟩ Creative corners

Finish the window and start building around the corner. This house's corners are made using bricks with side studs that will later have tiles attached to them. To make sure the corners are stable enough, build a layer of plates into each wall.

A plate above the window creates a level building surface with the wall sections next to it

MORE TILES FOR THE SIDES.

Place the plate layer five studs up the wall to stabilise the bricks below it

4 ⟩ Three walls

Build until you have constructed three matching walls, each the same width a with a window in the middle. Keep the centre wall one brick-level higher than two side-walls... for now! Next, attac brightly coloured tiles to the side studs the walls to make decorative brickwork

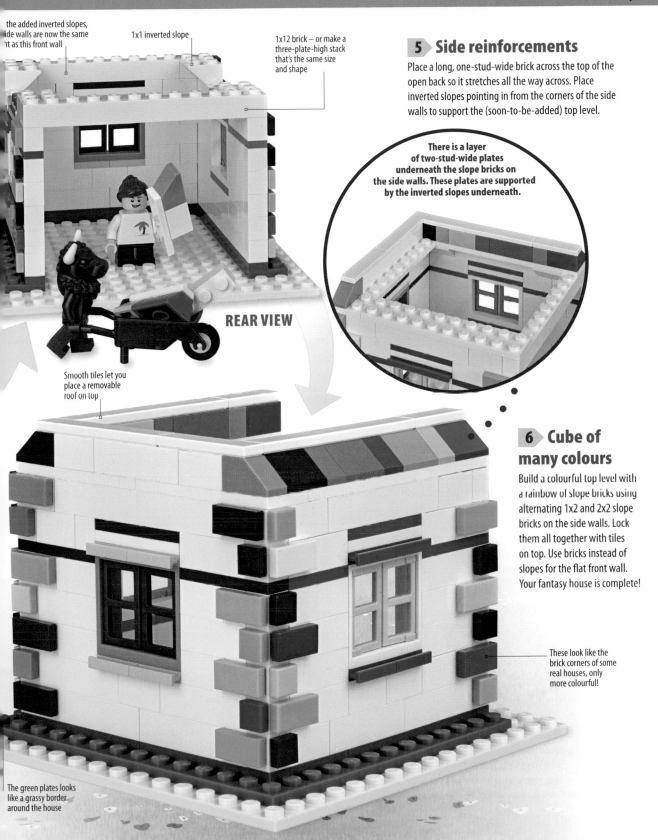

the added inverted slopes, ide walls are now the same t as this front wall

1x1 inverted slope

1x12 brick – or make a three-plate-high stack that's the same size and shape

5 Side reinforcements

Place a long, one-stud-wide brick across the top of the open back so it stretches all the way across. Place inverted slopes pointing in from the corners of the side walls to support the (soon-to-be-added) top level.

There is a layer of two-stud-wide plates underneath the slope bricks on the side walls. These plates are supported by the inverted slopes underneath.

REAR VIEW

Smooth tiles let you place a removable roof on top

6 Cube of many colours

Build a colourful top level with a rainbow of slope bricks using alternating 1x2 and 2x2 slope bricks on the side walls. Lock them all together with tiles on top. Use bricks instead of slopes for the flat front wall. Your fantasy house is complete!

These look like the brick corners of some real houses, only more colourful!

The green plates looks like a grassy border around the house

Cube village

Arranged around the cube house is a weird and wonderful village of similarly shaped homes, each one different from all of its neighbours. Use your bricks to make these colourful fantasy buildings, or custom-create your own new versions.

WHAT'S NEXT?

You've assembled one fantasy-land house. Now you can build more, in lots of varied and multicoloured styles.

Window canopy

This canopy is supported by two 1x2 inverted slopes in the wall. A 1x6 arch on top is locked into the wall by a 2x6 plate, with slopes forming an awning overhead.

MISMATCH HOUSE

A white 2x6 plate in the wall forms a base for six small half arches with matching 1x2 tiles to make this colourful striped awning.

A line of tiles tops the walls

Stripe is a 2x10 plate inside the wall

THE NEIGHBOURS' NEW PAINT JOB IS DELIGHTFUL.

Window attache bricks w

Mismatch house

This detailed little house is surrounded by flowers of multiple sizes. Each of its walls and windows is built in a different way, so you can see something new when you look at it from any angle.

Decorative pattern made from 1x2 textured bricks facing forward and backward

Flowers are stacks of 1x1 round plates, with flower plates at the bases

1x2 plates with handled alternate with 1x1 plates with side rings

Wall panels

The back of each panel on the house is made from regular bricks and bricks with side studs. A plate covered with slopes then attaches to the sideways studs.

Walls are two studs thick to make room for inset sections

There are colourful windowsills inside the building

REAR VIEW

The panel fits into this gap in the building frame

OUR HOUSE

Upper level built with 1x1 and 2x2 slopes

The wall panels on this side feature colorful 1x1 slopes

Colour house

From the front, this looks like a classic timber-framed wooden house. But its sides reveal an explosion of colour, thanks to a rainbow of slopes built into the walls and roof.

On this side, the 1x1 slopes are all the same tan colour

Scale house

With its scale-like shingled walls and rows of fang-like points, this house looks like a very civilised dragon might live here! Its corners are stacks of 2x2 crates, and flower boxes perch on its windowsills.

REAR VIEW

CALE HOUSE

Tooth plates attached using sideways building

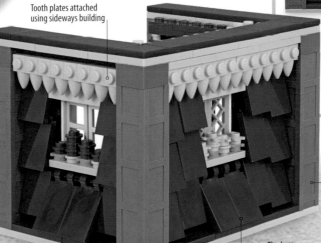

Shingle walls

Flag-like tiles attach to 1x2 plates with bars built into the wall, with two bricks between each bar-plate level.

Walls are three studs deep to make room for the angled shingles

The bottom row of shingles sticks out more than the rest

Fences and pathways

Alice departs the village of cube houses and her fantasy land stretches out before her. What path will she take and where will it lead her? She has lots of choices… and so do you!

These flowers are m
triple-scoop ice-cre

Build bricks with sideways-facing studs into the edges of your path to let you line it with flowers and plants.

Dirt track

This well-worn path is composed of many types of dirt. To make it, build a curvy wall out of bumpy log bricks, and then lay it down on its side.

Flower fence

Make a fence or wall look more inviting by building an arrangement of flowers on top. In a fantasy land, flowers can look like almost anything!

Staggered rows of 1x2 and 1x4 log bricks form a curved shape

Create random, irregular blocks of colour for natural-looking patches of earth

These double layers of plates hide and lock down the hinge plates

2x2 round tiles for big pathway stones

Build in texture with brick-patterned bric
textured bricks, log bricks and tiles attached to bricks with side studs

Candy cobblestones

In this land, pebbles and stones have the bright colours of candy buttons. A winding path becomes extra-winding when you build in hinges.

Hidden hinge plates in the path's corners let it move and shift.

Follow the pathway's shape with curved and angled plates

Stepped plates make the side ramps

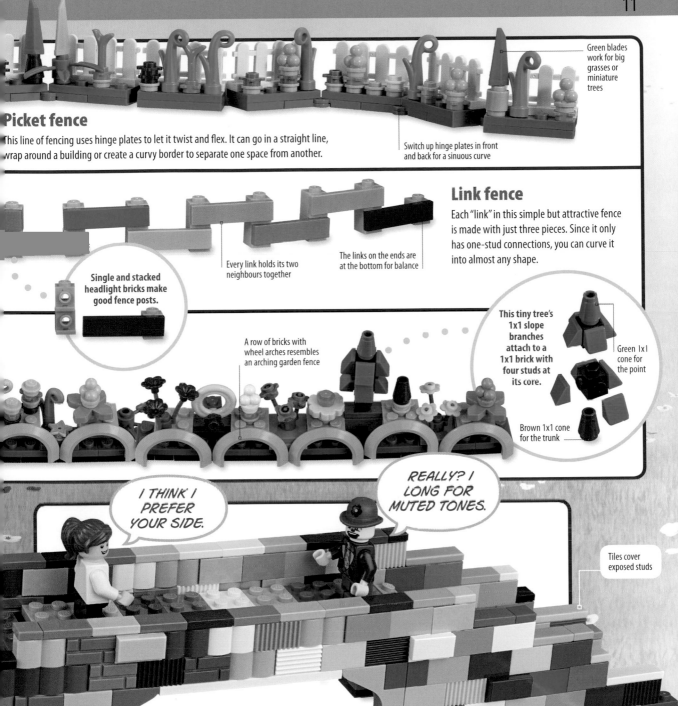

Picket fence

This line of fencing uses hinge plates to let it twist and flex. It can go in a straight line, wrap around a building or create a curvy border to separate one space from another.

Green blades work for big grasses or miniature trees

Switch up hinge plates in front and back for a sinuous curve

Link fence

Each "link" in this simple but attractive fence is made with just three pieces. Since it only has one-stud connections, you can curve it into almost any shape.

Single and stacked headlight bricks make good fence posts.

Every link holds its two neighbours together

The links on the ends are at the bottom for balance

This tiny tree's 1x1 slope branches attach to a 1x1 brick with four studs at its core.

Green 1x1 cone for the point

Brown 1x1 cone for the trunk

A row of bricks with wheel arches resembles an arching garden fence

Tiles cover exposed studs

I THINK I PREFER YOUR SIDE.

REALLY? I LONG FOR MUTED TONES.

Bridge

This bridge separates the real world from the land of fantasy. It has realistic colours and textures at one end, and fantastical ones at the other!

Arched elements for support

A waterfall

Building a long river could seem like a lengthy task, but you can build up a whole river by making it one smaller section at a time. This plunging waterfall is a model on its own, but it also forms the first part of a flowing fantasy river, which you'll find if you turn the page!

START HERE

Put the flat sides of two angled plates together for a diagonal base

1 ▶ River base

Make a flat base for your river model to rise up from, using angled plates for natural-looking curves and bends. Place a few similar bases end to end, and you've got the start of a river.

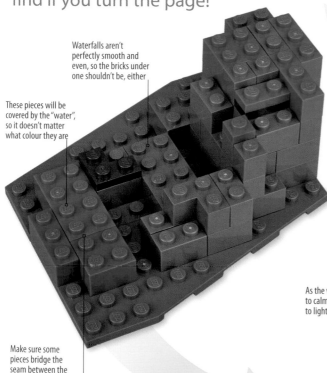

Waterfalls aren't perfectly smooth and even, so the bricks under one shouldn't be, either

These pieces will be covered by the "water", so it doesn't matter what colour they are

Make sure some pieces bridge the seam between the two angled plates, to lock them together

2 ▶ Rocky rise

Use bricks and plates to build up the river bottom, locking the base plates together. Since this river begins with a waterfall, create a tall brick structure at one end.

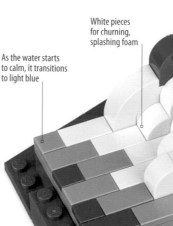

White pieces for churning, splashing foam

As the water starts to calm, it transitions to light blue

3 ▶ Falling water

The waterfall's plunging water is made using curved half-arch elements built up like steps. Use blue for the slow-moving water at the top, and white where it starts falling fast and getting all churned up.

Uneven arches make the water look more real

The water's exposed studs are hidden by tiles

Riverbank

ey slopes and bricks to form the
fall's rocky sides, and log bricks for
ked dirt riverbank. Leave the studs
top of these bricks exposed so
ppear extra rocky and uneven.

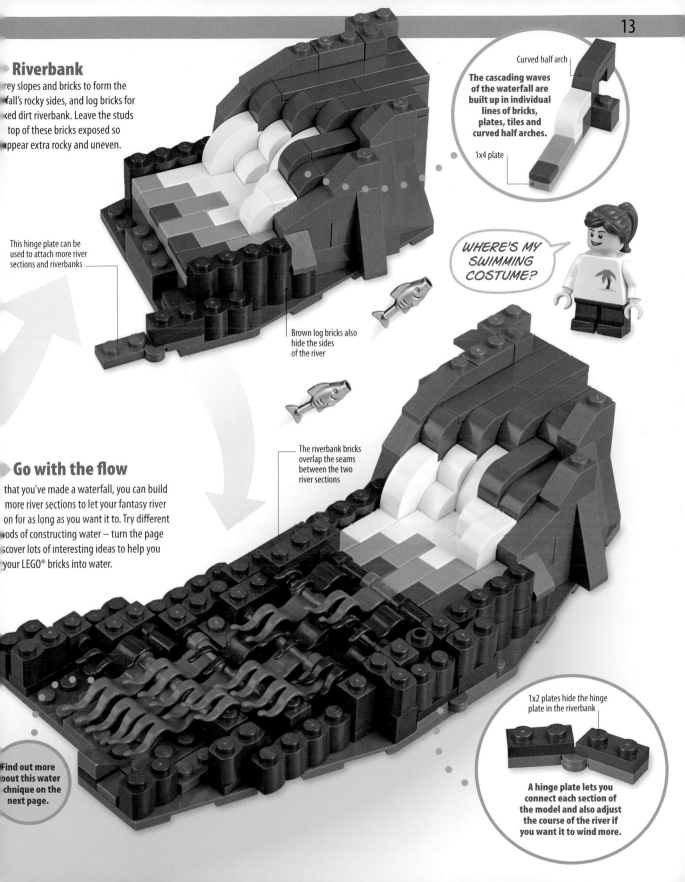

Curved half arch

**The cascading waves
of the waterfall are
built up in individual
lines of bricks,
plates, tiles and
curved half arches.**

1x4 plate

This hinge plate can be
used to attach more river
sections and riverbanks

Brown log bricks also
hide the sides
of the river

*WHERE'S MY
SWIMMING
COSTUME?*

The riverbank bricks
overlap the seams
between the two
river sections

Go with the flow

that you've made a waterfall, you can build
more river sections to let your fantasy river
on for as long as you want it to. Try different
ods of constructing water – turn the page
scover lots of interesting ideas to help you
your LEGO® bricks into water.

Find out more
bout this water
chnique on the
next page.

1x2 plates hide the hinge
plate in the riverbank

**A hinge plate lets you
connect each section of
the model and also adjust
the course of the river if
you want it to wind more.**

Fantasy river

There are many different ways to build water using your LEGO bricks, and in a fantasy land, one river can feature as many different water effects as you like – this ever-changing river features a few. Can you think of any more?

WHAT'S NEXT

Each section of the flowing fantasy river begins with the same angled-plate base as the waterfall on the previous page, with all kinds of bricks added to it to make a variety of water textures.

Go with the flow

This magical river changes from tranquil streams to raging rapids at every twist and turn. At each point where the river's building style changes, one hinge plate connects one section to the next.

I WON'T GET IN. IT'LL RUIN MY MAKEUP.

Curved slopes make choppy-looking waters

Rows of 1x1 slopes create short, sharp ripples in the water

Water wall

Make water look as still and clear as glass by building a wall of transparent blue bricks and then laying it down sideways in a matching-shaped space between the riverbank walls.

The streamers all point in the same direction

For fast-running water currents, slide blue streamer pieces onto poles or bars and plug them into riverbank bricks with hollow side studs.

'TIS THE BEST WAY TO KEEP ME CLOTHES CLEAN AND GREEN!

WHO DARES TO BATHE IN MY RIVER?

Use darker blue pieces for the deepest part of the river, and lighter blue for the shallow sides

The water gets bubbly here thanks to the studs on top of 2x2 and 1x1 transparent round plates

Smooth slope

To depict water flowing gently down a slope, you can layer smooth, transparent blue tiles with clips over blue bricks. Create a sloped shape by adding one or two plates underneath the blue bricks.

Lowering the brick by a plate's height leaves space for the clip

Fantasy creatures

As she walks through her fantasy forest, Alice encounters everything from giant butterflies to tiny, trilling dragons. What other marvellous and mystical creatures might you spy in your own fantasy forest?

Giant butterfly

Alice can hardly believe her eyes at this butterfly's size! It's big in real-brick scale, but compared to a minifigure, it's positively enormous. Use arches and slopes to give the wings their shapes, and bricks and plates to create one-of-a-kind wing patterns.

Antennae elements for antennae!

Make your butterflies whatever colours you want – the more vivid, the better!

A 1x2 plate locks the inverted curved slopes together

A half arch piece makes a scalloped edge

Bricks with vertical bars on the wings snap into pairs of clips built into the body

Butterfly body

Most of the butterfly's body is a stack of 1x2 plates and bricks, with 1x1 plates with clips to connect the handles on the wings. Small brackets at the front and back provide studs for attaching curved slopes on top.

Build bricks with round holes into the wings, then plug in the studs of 1x1 round bricks to make colourful 3-D details.

A clip-and-bar hinge attaches the pointed wing extension

Mini dragons

Build tiny dragons to inhabit your fantasy forest using small pieces with complementary colours. Attach the wings to clips so they can flap up and down.

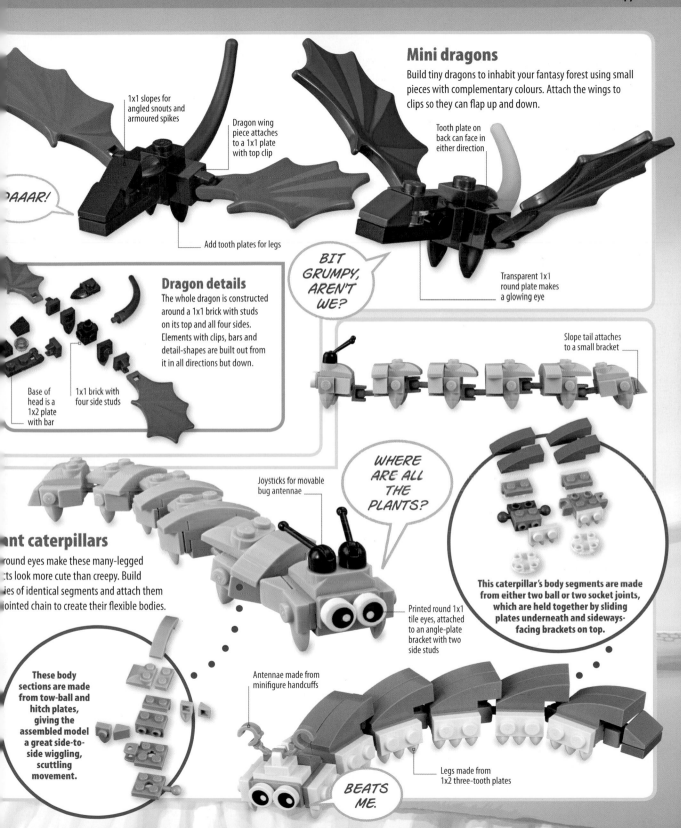

1x1 slopes for angled snouts and armoured spikes

Dragon wing piece attaches to a 1x1 plate with top clip

Add tooth plates for legs

Tooth plate on back can face in either direction

Transparent 1x1 round plate makes a glowing eye

AAAR!

BIT GRUMPY, AREN'T WE?

Dragon details

The whole dragon is constructed around a 1x1 brick with studs on its top and all four sides. Elements with clips, bars and detail-shapes are built out from it in all directions but down.

Base of head is a 1x2 plate with bar

1x1 brick with four side studs

Slope tail attaches to a small bracket

WHERE ARE ALL THE PLANTS?

This caterpillar's body segments are made from either two ball or two socket joints, which are held together by sliding plates underneath and sideways-facing brackets on top.

Giant caterpillars

round eyes make these many-legged cts look more cute than creepy. Build ies of identical segments and attach them ointed chain to create their flexible bodies.

Joysticks for movable bug antennae

Printed round 1x1 tile eyes, attached to an angle-plate bracket with two side studs

These body sections are made from tow-ball and hitch plates, giving the assembled model a great side-to-side wiggling, scuttling movement.

Antennae made from minifigure handcuffs

Legs made from 1x2 three-tooth plates

BEATS ME.

Tree slide

Imagine the fun things you can add to the trees of a fantasy forest. How about a fairy's home or a dragon's nest? Or a magical slide that takes you on a speedy, twisting trip down the tallest tree in the woods?

Crow's nest

At the top of the slide is a platform with railings, so you can look out and see the entire forest all around. It's built with three 4x4 quarter-circle plates and extra rectangular plates to make the spacing fit perfectly with the start of the slide.

Safety railings made from curved and straight fence pieces

1x2 tiles lock the railings together

The top of the slide sits level with the platform

1x1 cone for the tapered end of a branch

Leaves can be spread out around the tree, or clustered in dense bunches

Mix different leaf colours for

Building branches

Angled LEGO Technic connectors, held together by short cross axles, let you build the branches so that they grow in every direction, like those of a real tree. The leaf pieces are held on by bars, pushed into the tops of LEGO Technic pins with hollow studs.

Bricks with holes connect the branches to the trunk

LEGO® Technic pin connects the bar to the connector hole

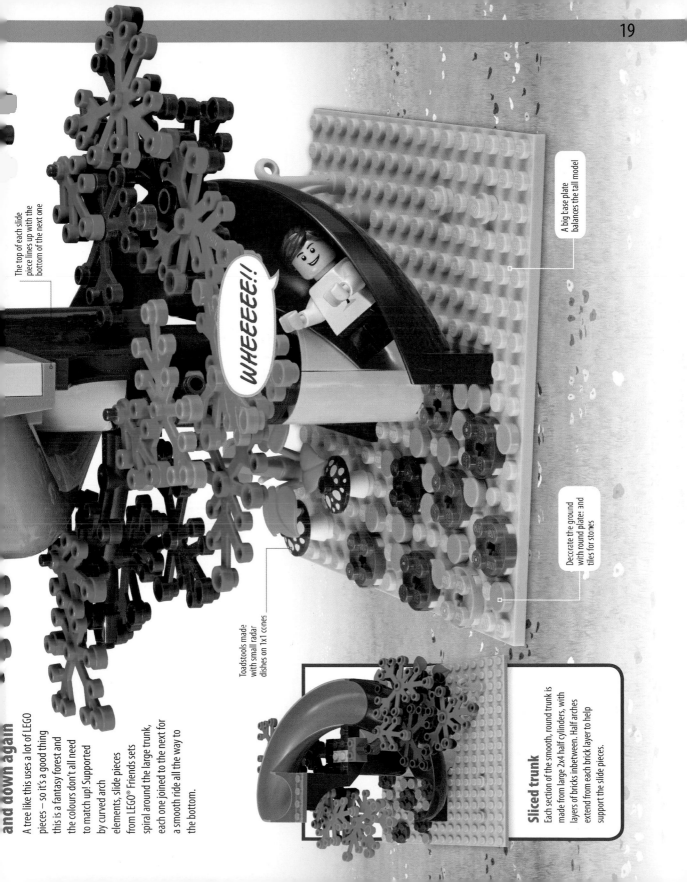

and down again

A tree like this uses a lot of LEGO pieces — so it's a good thing this is a fantasy forest and the colours don't all need to match up! Supported by curved arch elements, slide pieces from LEGO® Friends sets spiral around the large trunk, each one joined to the next for a smooth ride all the way to the bottom.

The top of each slide piece lines up with the bottom of the next one

A big base plate balances the tall model

Decorate the ground with round plate: and tiles for stones

Toadstools made with small radar dishes on 1x1 cones

WHEEEEE!!

Sliced trunk

Each section of the smooth, round trunk is made from large 2x4 half cylinders, with layers of bricks inbetween. Half arches extend from each brick layer to help support the slide pieces.

Tree-house

Use two curved railing pieces for a half-circle or one for a quarter-circle

Doorway leads to a slide

JUST MONKEYING AROUND.

In a very large tree in Alice's fantasy forest is a magnifice tree-house. It has been buil right into the mid of the tree, with its door at the base ar rooms that go all the way up its trun

Home in the woods

Use brown bricks and curved arches to buil a sturdy trunk for your tree-house. Suppor floors of the hollow spaces from undernea and secure your pieces together with lots interlocking plates so that they won't fa apart. Include some decorative touc like furnishings, terraces with rai and a stairway lined with flowe

Living room

At the bottom of the trunk is a cosy furnished room with a couch, bookshelf, drawers and a sink. The patterned floor mixes smooth tiles with 2x2 jumpe plates that have studs where minifigures can stanc

The modular tree

Each of the tree's three sections is built separately. Their tops are lined with tiles with just a couple of studs, so that they can be taken apart and played with or moved around.

The brick walls of the trunk are staggered to make it stable

Branches made from LEGO Technic connectors, 1x1 cones and leaf elements connected by pins and bars

Each flowerpot attaches to a 1x2 jumper plate on top of a 1x2 brick

Small staircase made of 1x4 plates with one stud at each end leads up to the balcony

Staggered inverted arches create realistic root shapes

A stone path made from round plates and tiles leads to the front door

EXPLODED VIEW

A castle wall

Bonk! What could Alice have just walked into? Why, it's the wall of a grand castle! Start your own fantasy castle by building a rainbow-coloured wall, with connectors on the sides so that it can attach to other walls with the same design.

START HERE

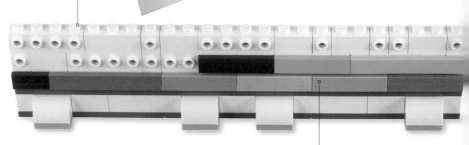

The plates lock the bricks above and below them together

Curved bricks make smooth and stud-free feet

1 > **Fantastic foundation**

How do you build a strong standing wall? Begin with a solid, two-stud-wide foundation base made of bricks... and add feet so it won't fall over! Plate layers provide attractive stripes.

2 > **Studs and tiles**

Build up the wall with one-stud-wide bricks. Include bricks with studs on their sides, all pointing in the same direction, so that you can decorate the front and leave the back plain. Snap coloured tiles onto the studs in a staggered pattern.

You can use 1x1, 1x2 or 1x4 bricks with side studs

Make sure each tile is attached to at least two studs so it won't fall off

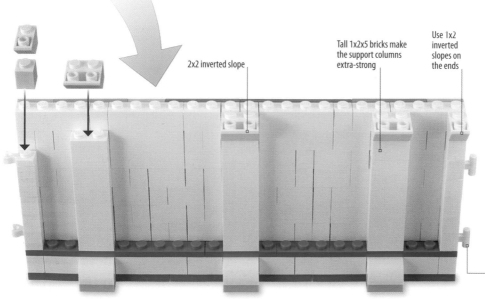

2x2 inverted slope

Tall 1x2x5 bricks make the support columns extra-strong

Use 1x2 inverted slopes on the ends

3 > **Supports and modular connect**

At the back of the wall, stack up bricks into columns above each rear-facing foot, topping them inverted slopes. Build similar 1x stacks at each edge, incorporati plates with clips on one end an with handled bars on the other.

Line up the clips and handles so they would snap together if you had two matching walls next to each other

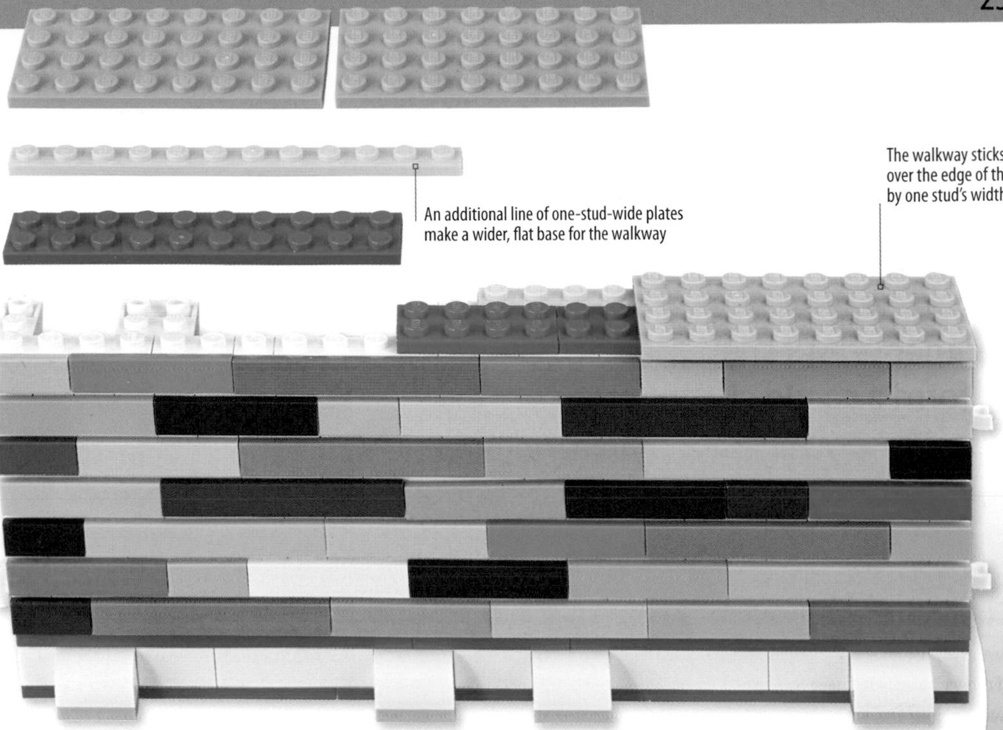

Wall-top
Walkway

...down a layer of plates
...ck the bricks at the top
...e wall together with
...upport columns'
...ted slopes. On top
...s layer, attach a line
...ur-stud-wide plates to
...e a wide walkway.

**...ESE DEFENSES
BETTER BE
...CURE, BUILDER!**

An additional line of one-stud-wide plates make a wider, flat base for the walkway

The walkway sticks out over the edge of the wall by one stud's width

You could cover the walkway with tiles, but studs will let you attach minifigures

For a more realistic stone wall, substitute grey tiles for the rainbow-hued ones shown here. Use a variety of grey shades as different types of stones.

The studs on the parapet resemble the stone blocks of real castle battlements

5 Parapet

As a final touch, add a short parapet wall of one-stud-wide bricks along the front edge of the walkway. Now the castle's guards won't fall over the edge — and they have something to duck down behind if enemies attack!

More castle walls

With the clips and handles on the sides of your wall, you can build multiple segments and snap them together to form a castle circumference of any size. Make your walls match, or mix things up with these fanciful designs.

WHAT'S NEXT?

Each of these walls starts on the same foundation as the one on the previous pages. The difference lies in how you build it up from there!

Cupboard wall

You've probably heard of a chest of drawers, but how about an entire wall of them? This wall alternates one-stud-wide brick columns with opening LEGO drawer and cabinet elements. It's the perfect place to stow your treasures or your spare carrots!

A parapet of curved slopes on top

You don't have to cover the whole wall with drawers – a couple of gaps add depth and visual interest

Use tall column bricks or stacks of shorter ones

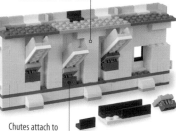

Double-thickness sections reinforce the wall

Chutes attach to two-part hinges

REAR VIEW

4x4 plate with hole

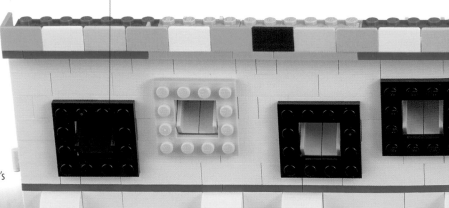

Chute wall

The slide-like chutes on this wall let your castle's defenders roll stones onto hostile attackers... or send food down to beloved pets. Build them with small wall panels on plates, held at an angle by a snap-together hinge.

Arch wall

The white bricks of this wall are built one row of studs back on the foundation base, making room for a lattice-like pattern of curved half-arch elements. The parapet rail on top is made from smaller half arches with a similar curved shape.

Make all of your arches the same colour, or combine different colours

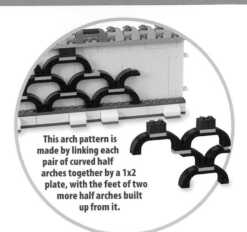

This arch pattern is made by linking each pair of curved half arches together by a 1x2 plate, with the feet of two more half arches built up from it.

1x1 flower plate decoration

Use 1x1 round or square plates to connect arches at the wall's edge

Curved half arches locked together by 1x2 tile form defensive battlements

Each "bump" on this woven wall is made from curved slope bricks locked together with a plate underneath.

Use curved slopes of different lengths to make longer or shorter "bumps"

Woven wall

This wall uses curved slopes to make rounded stripe shapes. They're attached to sideways-built plates and staggered to resemble the texture of a woven straw basket.

Castle walls (continued)

Build the colour bricks into a second wall behind the first one – make sure you lock both walls together securely!

Window-frame wall

Empty white window frames of different shapes and sizes, w blocks of coloured bricks behind them, make this wall look li the artwork of painter Piet Mondrian. A smooth walkway wi a latticed parapet enhances its classic-yet-colourful style.

White bricks fill the spaces between window frames

Frames can be squares or long or tall rectangles

Create a staggered tile design by lining up bricks with side studs in even rows, then attaching the tiles at either their top or bottom.

Connect long tiles to inverted 1x2 brackets for the parapet wall

Tiled wall

Make a tiled pattern by attaching 2x2 square tiles onto rows of bricks with side studs built into your wall. For extra texture and variety, sprinkle in a bunch of 2x2 jumper plates with central studs, too.

Wall indented by one stud

WHAT'S THE PASSWORD?

Railing made from tiles attached to 1x1 bricks with side studs

To connect the baskets, build a plate layer into the wall and leave some one-stud-wide gaps for the basket hole to fit onto.

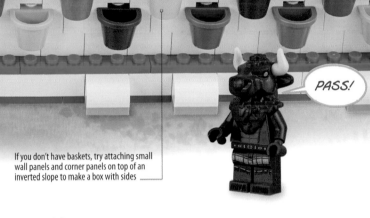

Flowerpot wall

Here's a new idea: a castle wall decorated with flowerpots! Space the baskets apart so that there is room to place small accessories inside. Fill them with flowers, or put something different into each one.

PASS!

If you don't have baskets, try attaching small wall panels and corner panels on top of an inverted slope to make a box with sides

Arches go over the wall panels

Short inverted slope

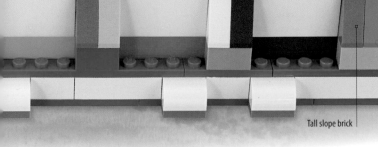

Paneled wall

This wall design makes use of LEGO castle wall panels with cut-out windows, and places slope elements between them for structural bracing. Bigger at the bottom and smaller at the top, the braces add stability and support the top walkway.

Tall slope brick

Castle features

What other features besides towers and catapults can you add to your fantasy castle? You could build a grand entrance archway to welcome new visitors to the kingdom… or decorate your castle courtyard with a dazzling ice-cream cone fountain!

While you could build your own arches out of smaller pieces, using a single arch-shaped element will make your model stronger and able to support more weight.

1x2 brick w axle hole

1x1 flower plate on a 1x1 round brick

Grooved pattern made with the fronts and backs of 1x2 textured bricks

Climbing vines are leaf elements attached to bricks with side studs

For a cobbled castle floor, place a variety of round grey and brown plates and tiles on top of grey plates

Slope bricks create a wider and sturdier base for the gatehouse wall

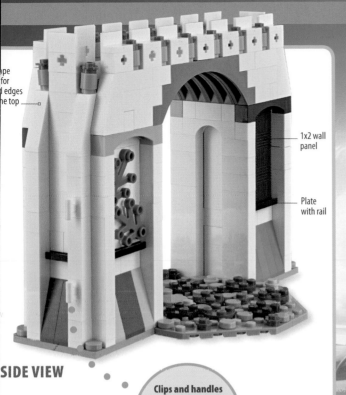

...pe
for
edges
the top

1x2 wall
panel

Plate
with rail

SIDE VIEW

Clips and handles on the sides of the gatehouse can connect to the castle wall models and castle towers.

Gatehouse arch

A gatehouse provides a way for friends to pass through the castle's high wall. Build it to be tall and wide so that riders and wagons can go through, too. Add interesting features to enliven its flat sides, and detail the ground underneath with dirt and stones.

WISH EVERY DAY WAS CHOCOLATE FOUNTAIN DAY.

The bottom of the axle plugs into a 2x2 round brick to connect it to the fountain base

Ice-cream fountain

The fountain's ice-cream-scoop top is built with four quarter-dome pieces on a 6x6 round plate. It is supported by a stack of two 2x2 round bricks and a plate, which are pushed onto a long LEGO Technic axle and hidden inside a tan-coloured drill for a cone.

This fountain's ice-cream cone shape is no coincidence — on festival days, it sprays ice cream instead of water!

Fountain

Whether ornately elegant or festive and fun, a fountain can really brighten up a fantasy castle's courtyard and other open spaces. There are hundreds of ways to build one. Start with a wall around a water-filled base, then add a high spout in the middle.

Use blue for water, or add coloured pieces inside the fountain wall to represent different ice-cream flavours

4x4 curved plates for a base

Curved wall made with large macaroni bricks

Life is always colourful in this fantasy land.

I BE WINGIN' ME WAY TO A POT O' GOLD!

THIS PLACE IS A REGULAR CIRCUS.

HERE, TAKE THE PIE!

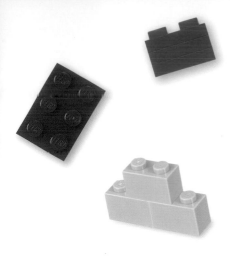

DK | Penguin Random House

Senior Editor Hannah Dolan
Editors Natalie Edwards, Matt Jones, Helen Leech, Clare Millar, Rosie Peet
Senior Cover Designer Mark Penfound
Senior Designers Anthony Limerick, David McDonald, Lisa Sodeau
Project Art Editor Lauren Adams
Designers Thelma Jane-Robb, Gema Salamanca, Abi Wright
Design Assistant Ellie Bilbow
Pre-Production Producer Kavita Varma
Senior Producer Kathleen McNally
Managing Editor Paula Regan
Design Managers Jo Connor, Guy Harvey
Creative Manager Sarah Harland
Publisher Julie Ferris
Art Director Lisa Lanzarini
Publishing Director Simon Beecroft

Models built by Yvonne Doyle, Alice Finch, Rod Gillies, Tim Goddard,
Tim Johnson, Barney Main, Drew Maughan and Pete Reid
Photography by Gary Ombler

Dorling Kindersley would like to thank Randi Sørensen, Henk van der Does, Melody Caddick,
Alexandra Martin, Heike Bornhausen, Paul Hansford, Robert Ekblom and Lisbeth Finnemann
Skrumsager at the LEGO Group. Thanks also to Pamela Afram, Beth Davies, Andy Jones, Keifer
Lewin-Nation and Scarlett O'Hara at DK for editorial assistance and Jon Hall, Pamela Shiels,
Rhys Thomas and Jade Wheaton for design assistance.

First published in Great Britain in 2017 by
Dorling Kindersley Limited 80 Strand, London, WC2R 0RL

Contains content previously published in LEGO® *Awesome Ideas* (2015)

001–310867–Oct/17

www.LEGO.com
www.dk.com

A WORLD OF IDEAS:
SEE ALL THERE IS TO KNOW